¿Cómo está el tiempo hoy?

What Is the Weather Like Today?

School Specialty Publishing

Publicado por School Specialty Publishing, un miembro de School Specialty Family.

©℗ 2007 Twin Sisters IP, LLC. Todos los derechos reservados.

Envíe sus preguntas a:
School Specialty Publishing
8720 Orion Place
Columbus, OH 43240-2111 USA

Créditos:

Productores ejecutivos: Kim Mitzo Thompson, Karen Mitzo Hilderbrand
Ilustrado por: Dorothy Stott
Diseñado por: Angelee Randlett
Publicado por: Twin Sisters Productions, LLC
Narrado por: Austin Thompson, Morgan Thompson (Ingles)
            Norberto Monarrez Jr., Kimberly Capilla (Español)
Traducido por: Carol A. Trexler
La música por: Hal Wright
Escrito por: Kim Mitzo Thompson

ISBN: 0-7696-4617-4
EAN   9-780769-64617-6+50499
UPC: 0-87577-92317-8+04617

¿Cómo está el tiempo hoy?

Está soleado.

¿Cómo está el tiempo hoy?

Hace calor.

¿Cómo está el tiempo hoy?

Está nublado.

¿Cómo está el tiempo hoy?

Está lloviendo.

¿Cómo está el tiempo hoy?

Hay viento.

¿Cómo está el tiempo hoy?

Está nevando.

¿Cómo está el tiempo hoy?

Hace frío.

The weather
El tiempo

Today
Hoy

Cold
Frío

Snowing
Nevando

Windy
Viento

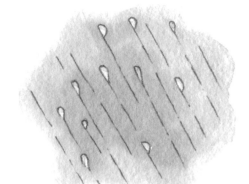

Raining
Lloviendo

Nublado
Cloudy

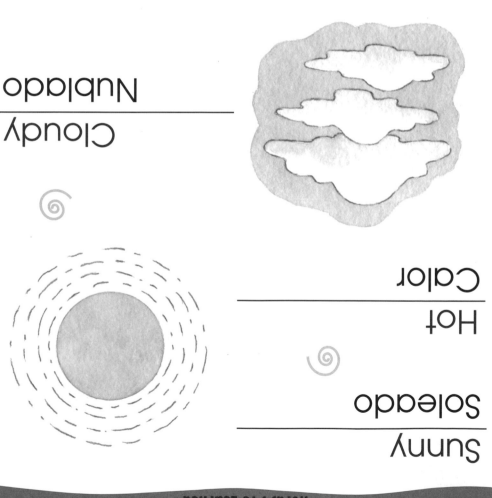

Calor
Hot

Soleado
Sunny

It is cold.

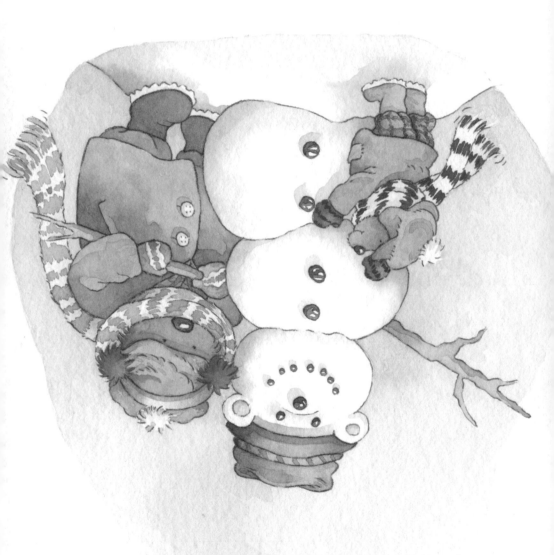

What is the weather like today?

It is snowing.

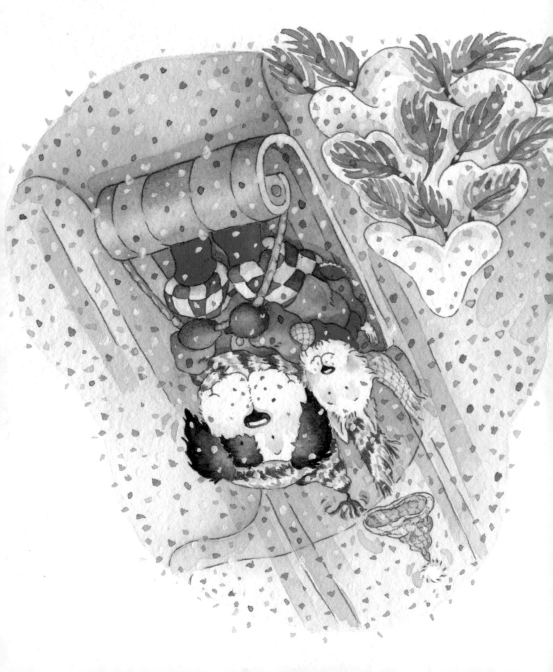

What is the weather like today?

It is windy.

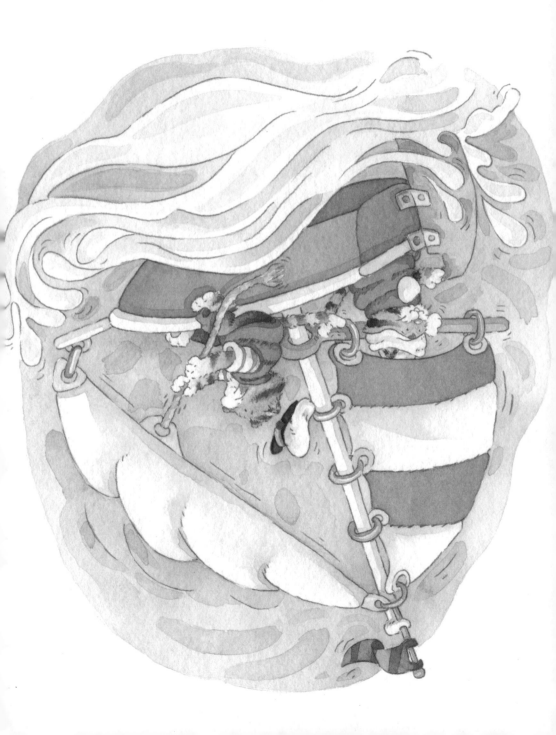

What is the weather like today?

It is raining.

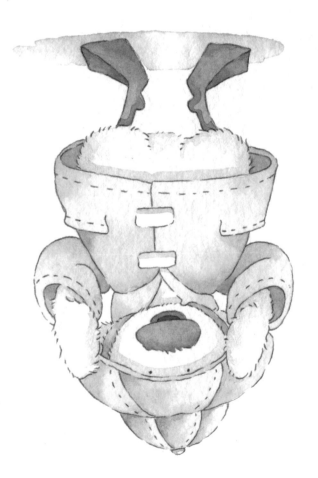

It is cloudy.

What is the weather like today?

It is hot.

What is the weather like today?

It is sunny.

What is the weather like today?

What Is the Weather Like Today?
¿Cómo está el tiempo hoy?

Published by School Specialty Publishing, a member of the School Specialty Family.

Send inquiries to:
School Specialty Publishing
8720 Orion Place
Columbus, Ohio 43240-2111

Credits:

Executive Producers: Kim Mitzo Thompson, Karen Mitzo Hilderbrand

Illustrated by: Dorothy Stott

Designed by: Angelee Randlett

Published by: Twin Sisters Productions, LLC

Readers: Austin Thompson, Morgan Thompson (English)
Norberto Monarrez Jr., Kimberly Capilla (Spanish)

Translated by: Carol A. Trexler

Music by: Hal Wright

Written By: Kim Mitzo Thompson

ISBN: 0-7696-4617-4
EAN: 9-780769-646176
UPC: 0-87577-92317-8+04617